EXPLORING NATURE
TURTLES
& TORTOISES

An in-depth look at chelonians, the shelled reptiles
that have existed since the time of the dinosaurs

Barbara Taylor
Consultants: Andy and Nadine Highfield
The Tortoise Trust

ARMADILLO

C O N

This edition is published by Armadillo,
an imprint of Anness Publishing Ltd

www.annesspublishing.com
Twitter: @Anness_Books

Anness Publishing has a picture agency outlet
for images for publishing, promotions or
advertising. Please visit our website
www.practicalpictures.com for more
information.

Publisher: Joanna Lorenz
Project Editors: Laura Seber, Richard McGinlay
Designer: Linda Penny
Picture Researcher: Su Alexander
Illustrator: John Francis
Maps: Anthony Duke
Production Controller: Rosanna Anness

PUBLISHER'S NOTE
Although the advice and information in this
book are believed to be accurate and true at the
time of going to press, neither the authors nor
the publisher can accept any legal responsibility
or liability for any errors or omissions that may
have been made.

Manufacturer: Anness Publishing Ltd,
108 Great Russell Street, London WC1B 3NA,
England
For Product Tracking go to:
www.annesspublishing.com/tracking
Batch: 6792-23456-1127

T E N T S

What Are Turtles and Tortoises?

Turtles, tortoises and terrapins make up a group of reptiles called chelonians. They have lived on the Earth for more than 220 million years, since the days of the earliest dinosaurs.

There are about 300 different kinds of chelonian, living in warm places all over the world. Those types that live in the sea are called turtles. Other types of chelonian have different names in different countries. In the UK, for example, those that live on land are tortoises, and those that live in fresh water are called terrapins. In the USA, however, most freshwater chelonians are called turtles, while in Australia they are called tortoises.

▲ OCEAN FLYERS

The green sea turtle is the largest of the sea turtles with hard shells. There are seven types of sea turtle, and they all have flattened, streamlined shells and powerful front flippers. They 'fly' gracefully through the water but move clumsily on land, and cannot pull their head and neck back into the shell as many land chelonians can.

STAR TURN ▼

With its high, domed shell, this Indian star tortoise looks like a walking tank. Only the head, legs and tail stick out of the shell, which has a top and a bottom part and goes right around the body. The stumpy legs are strong, like an elephant's, to support its weight. Land chelonians usually have these pillar-like legs. Those that live in water usually have webbed toes or flippers.

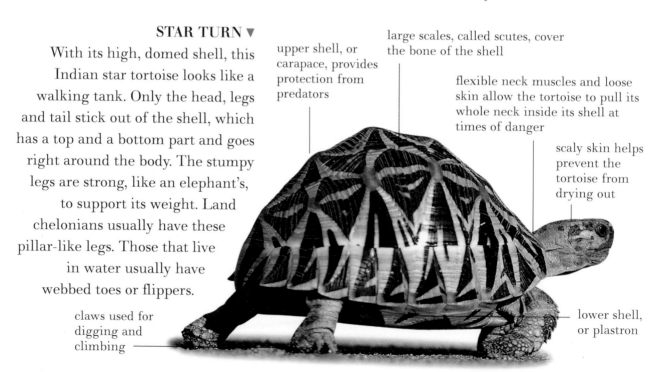

upper shell, or carapace, provides protection from predators

large scales, called scutes, cover the bone of the shell

flexible neck muscles and loose skin allow the tortoise to pull its whole neck inside its shell at times of danger

scaly skin helps prevent the tortoise from drying out

claws used for digging and climbing

lower shell, or plastron

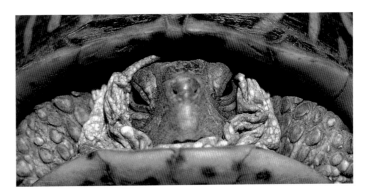

Turtle Who Taught Us

In the children's book Alice's Adventures in Wonderland, *by Lewis Carroll, Alice meets a character called the Mock Turtle, who is often upset and cries easily. He tells Alice a story about his school days, when he had an old turtle as a teacher. Alice is puzzled as to why the old turtle was called Tortoise. The Mock Turtle explains that the teacher was called Tortoise because he 'taught us'.*

▲ STRAIGHT BACK OR SIDES

Chelonians are divided into two groups according to the way they tuck their head inside their shell. Some fold the neck straight back on itself in a tight S-shape (top). The others bend their neck sideways under the lip of the top shell, leaving the neck and head slightly exposed at the front (bottom).

▼ TASTY TERRAPIN

The diamond-backed terrapin lives in the shallow marshes along North America's Atlantic coast, where fresh water and salt water mix together. For a hundred years or so, this terrapin was hunted for its tasty meat. Much of its habitat was also destroyed, and the terrapin almost became extinct. Today, thanks to conservation and changes in eating habits, numbers are recovering.

▲ BRAVE NEW WORLD

All chelonians lay shelled eggs on land, even those that live in the sea. This is because the young need to breathe oxygen from the air. When the baby chelonian is ready to hatch, it uses an egg tooth on its snout to cut through the shell. The egg tooth is a hard scale, not a real tooth. Even with the help of the egg tooth, escaping from the shell is a slow process.

▲ LAND TORTOISES

Land tortoises, such as this leopard tortoise, belong to the family Testudinidae. This is the second largest family, with more than 50 species, living mainly in hot areas of Africa, India, South-east Asia and South America. A few species live in cooler areas of southern Europe, western Asia and southern North America. The land tortoise family includes the giant tortoises of the Galapagos Islands and Aldabra. Land tortoises generally have a domed, bony shell and strong, stocky legs equipped with claws for digging. They eat mainly plants.

Familiar Faces

There are hundreds of different kinds, or species, of chelonian. These are grouped into twelve families, based on the features that they have in common. The biggest of these families has about 90 species, but four families contain only one species because there are no other chelonians that are quite like them. Chelonians such as land tortoises and sea turtles may be quite familiar to you. The largest and smallest chelonians belong to these families. The largest is the leatherback sea turtle, which tips the scales at 680kg (1,500lb) or more, while the tiny speckled padloper tortoise weighs less than 220g (9oz) and would easily fit on your hand.

SEA TURTLES ▶

Six species of hard-shelled sea turtle belong to the Cheloniidae family. These are the hawksbill (right), green, flatback, loggerhead, Kemp's Ridley and olive Ridley turtles. The giant leatherback turtle, with its soft, leathery shell, is so unusual that it is placed in a separate family. Sea turtles spend most of their lives in the ocean, but females lay their eggs on land. Their legs are shaped like flippers, and they cannot pull their head and neck back inside their shell.

POND TURTLES ▶

This slider, or red-eared terrapin, belongs to the largest and most varied group of chelonians, the Emydidae. There are more than 90 species in this family of pond turtles, members of which live on all continents except Australia and Antarctica. The top shell is shaped like a low arch, and some species have a movable hinge in the bottom shell. The legs of pond turtles are developed for swimming, and some are slightly webbed between the toes.

◀ POND TURTLE GROUPS

The pond turtle family, the Emydidae, is divided into two smaller subfamilies. The Batagurinae live in Europe, Africa and Asia. The Indian black turtle (left) belongs to this group, as does the spiny turtle, the Asian leaf turtle and the European pond turtle. The other group, the Emydinae, lives in parts of North, Central and South America. It includes species such as the slider, the spotted turtle, the wood turtle, the ornate box turtle and the painted turtle.

Did you know? The green turtle is named after its green body fat.

MUD OR MUSK TURTLES ▼

Members of the mud or musk turtle family, including the loggerhead musk turtle (below), live in an area ranging from Canada to South America. These small chelonians are named after the musky-smelling substances they produce when they are disturbed. These strong smells drive away any enemies. These turtles live in fresh water and one of their special characteristics is webs between their toes. Their legs are specially adapted for crawling along the muddy bottom of marshes, swamps and rivers. The bottom shell may have one or two movable hinges.

Strange Species

Did you know that there is a turtle with a face like a pig? This is just one of the many strange and surprising species of chelonians. They include the formidable snapping turtles and unusual softshells, and a turtle with a head too big for its own shell. There are also the strange side-necked turtles, which bend their neck sideways under their shell. Side-necked turtles were more common in the past, and one extinct species may have been the largest freshwater turtle that ever lived. It grew to a length of 230cm (90in), which is twice as long as the largest side-necked turtle alive today – the Arrau river turtle.

▲ SNAPPING TURTLES

The two types of the North American snapping turtle are the only chelonians that can be dangerous to people. They are named after their powerful, snapping jaws, and have terrible tempers when provoked, which makes them very hard to handle. The bottom shell of snapping turtles is small and shaped like a cross, which makes it easier for them to move their legs in muddy water and among thick water plants.

Did you know? Pig-nosed turtles in Australia have been known to eat giant fruit bats.

▼ SOFTSHELL TURTLES

The 22 species of softshell turtle have a flattened top shell covered with a leathery skin instead of a hard, horny covering. Their aggressive nature makes up to some extent for the poor protection given by their softer shells. Softshell turtles are agile, expert swimmers, with legs like paddles. The tip of their nose is a long tube with the nostrils at the very end. This means they can stay under water and breathe by just pushing their nostrils above the water's surface. Softshell turtles live in Africa, Asia and North America.

◀ BIG-HEADED TURTLE

The unique big-headed turtle is the only member of its family, Platysternidae. Its huge head is almost half the width of its top shell, far too big to be drawn back inside the shell. The skull has a solid bony roof for protection, and the head is covered by an extra-tough horny layer. Living in cool mountain streams in South-east Asia, the big-headed turtle comes out at night to catch small fish and other water creatures in its hooked jaws.

PIG-NOSED TURTLE ▼

The weird pig-nosed turtle has a snout that sticks out, like softshell turtles, but its nose is shorter, wrinkled and has the nostrils at the side, making it look like a pig. Another extraordinary feature is its front legs, which look like the flippers of sea turtles. The pig-nosed turtle lives in the rivers and lakes of Papua New Guinea and northern Australia. One river it inhabits is called the Fly River, so it is also named the Fly River turtle. It is the only member of the Carettochelyidae family.

◀ SIDE-NECKED TURTLES

There are about 60 species of side-necked turtles, such the yellow-spotted Amazon River turtle (left). Some of them have such long necks that they are called snake-necked turtles. Side-necked turtles are divided into two groups. One group, Pelomedusidae, lives only in South America, Africa and on some of the Indian Ocean islands. The other group, Chelidae, inhabits South America and the Australian region. They all live in freshwater habitats, such as streams, rivers, lakes and swamps, and their back feet are strongly webbed for swimming.

Focus on

The world's largest tortoises all live on islands – the Galapagos Islands in the Pacific Ocean and the coral atoll of Aldabra in the Indian Ocean. The Galapagos tortoises are up to 130cm (50in) long, and they can weigh 275kg (605lb) – that is as heavy as three men. It is likely that these giant tortoises reached the islands by floating over the ocean on rafts of plants or debris. The Aldabra tortoise probably came from Madagascar, while the Galapagos tortoises came from the mainland of South America.

SWIMMING LESSONS

Aldabra tortoises sometimes swim out to sea. This one is just climbing up the beach after swimming. In the water, the tortoise bobs up and down among the waves like a cork but does not swim very well.

SHELL SHAPES

Twelve species of giant tortoise live on the Galapagos Islands. These probably all evolved from a common ancestor, but each species then adapted to the different conditions on the different islands. For example, the shells of each species have a certain shape and thickness according to the habitat in which they live. Tortoises that live on the large and wet islands have thick, domed shells. On the smaller islands, which are drier and have fewer plants growing on them, the giant tortoises have long necks and legs and a shell that turns upwards behind the neck like a horse's saddle. This 'saddleback' shell (left) allows the tortoises to stretch their necks upwards to feed on taller plants, so they can collect enough food. The word *galapagos* is an old Spanish word for a kind of saddle that is turned up at the front, like the shells of the saddleback tortoises.

Island Giants

LITTLE AND LARGE
This Aldabra tortoise looks absolutely vast next to the world's smallest tortoise, a speckled padloper (roadwalker), or Cape tortoise. The speckled padloper has a shell as small as 10cm (4in) long, whereas the Aldabra tortoise has a shell up to 105cm (40in) long and weighs as much as 120kg (265lb).

TORTOISE COMPETITION
During the breeding season, male Galapagos tortoises are noisy while they are courting females, making loud roaring noises. They are also aggressive towards other males, charging and butting them with their heads. Saddleback males even have neck-stretching contests, to see which of them can reach the highest.

BATH-TIME
These giant Galapagos tortoises are soaking themselves in a muddy pool. This helps them to cool down, because large tortoises cannot lose heat as efficiently as smaller ones. Compared with the large volume of their bodies, the giants have a relatively small surface area through which their body heat can escape. Soaking in pools may also help the tortoises to get rid of ticks, mites and other parasites living on the outside of their bodies.

The Turtle Shell

No other animal has body protection quite like a chelonian's shell. The shell shields the animal from the weather and also from predators, and it will regrow if it is damaged. It also supports soft muscles and organs, such as the heart and lungs, inside the body. The shell is made of bony plates, which are covered by giant scales called scutes. Land chelonians typically have high-domed or knobbly shells to protect them from predators. Water chelonians have lighter, streamlined shells.

▲ TOPS AND BOTTOMS

Every turtle shell has a top part, known as the carapace, and a bottom part, the plastron. You can clearly see these on this upside-down Florida box turtle. The two parts of the shell are locked together on each side by bony bridges.

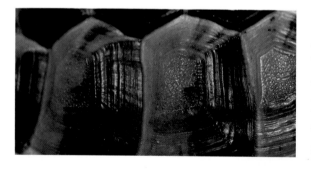

◄ HOW OLD?

Many chelonians have growth rings on their scutes. The rings represent a period of slow growth, such as during a dry season. It is not a very reliable method, however, to work out the age of a chelonian by counting the rings, because more than one ring may form in a year, and some rings may be worn away.

SOFTSHELLS ►

Named after their soft, leathery shells, softshell turtles also have a bony shell underneath. The bones have air spaces in them, which help the turtle float in water. Their flat shells make it easier for softshells to hide in soft mud and sand as they lie in wait for their prey.

▲ SHELL PROBLEMS

This young marginated tortoise has a deformed shell because it has been fed on the wrong food. Pet chelonians should be given mineral and vitamin supplements as well as the correct food in order to keep them healthy.

▲ FLAT AS A PANCAKE

The shell of the African pancake tortoise lives up to its name, being much flatter than those of other land species. This allows the tortoise to squeeze into narrow crevices under rocks to avoid predators and the hot sun. The flexible carapace also helps with this, and the tortoises use their legs and claws to fix themselves firmly in position. Once the tortoise has wedged itself in between the rocks, it is extremely difficult to remove it.

Turtle World
Turtle shells are very strong. The strongest ones can support a weight over 200 times heavier than the body of the turtle – that's like you having nine cars on your back! According to Hindu beliefs, the Earth is supported by four elephants standing on the back of a turtle that is floating in the Universal Ocean.

▲ TURTLE IN A BOX

Some chelonians, such as this box turtle, have a hinge on the plastron. This allows them to pull the head, legs and tail inside and shut the shell completely. In some species, this gives protection from predators, but protection against loss of moisture may also be important. African hinge-back tortoises have a hinge on the carapace rather than on the plastron.

13

How the Body Works

Chelonians have a skeleton both inside and outside their bodies. There is the bony shell on the outside, and on the inside there is a bony skeleton made up of the skull, backbone and ribs, and the leg, hip and shoulder bones.

Just like humans, chelonians use oxygen from the air to work their muscles, and this gets into the blood through the lungs. When we breathe in, our chest moves out to draw air into our lungs, but chelonians' ribs are fused to their shell, so they cannot expand their chest in this way. Instead, they use muscles between the front legs to force air in and out of the body.

scute

spine bones

carapace

plastron

▲ SPECIAL SKELETON
The shell of a chelonian is its outside skeleton, while inside the body is a framework of bones that provides an anchor for the muscles and protects the delicate internal organs. Apart from in the leatherback turtle, the spine bones and ribs are fused to the carapace (the top part of the shell).

SWIMMING BONES ▼
The most obvious features of a sea turtle's skeleton are the extremely long toe bones that support the front flippers. The toe bones of the back feet are also long and slim. Chelonians have eight neck bones (mammals have seven) and between 40 and 50 bones in their backbone (you have 33 of these bones). You can see how the shoulder and hip bones fit inside the ribs so the shell can cover the whole body. Most other animals have their shoulder and hip bones outside their ribs.

hip bones

shoulder bones

WINDOW ON THE BODY ▶

If you could see inside a chelonian's body, you would be able to see its heart, lungs and other internal organs. A three-chambered heart pumps the blood around the body. (Most reptiles have hearts with three chambers, while mammals, have four heart chambers.) The digestive system works fairly slowly, and food takes days to pass through the body. The digestive, excretory and reproductive systems all end in one chamber called the cloaca.

The hole where the cloaca opens to the outside may be called the cloaca, anus or vent.

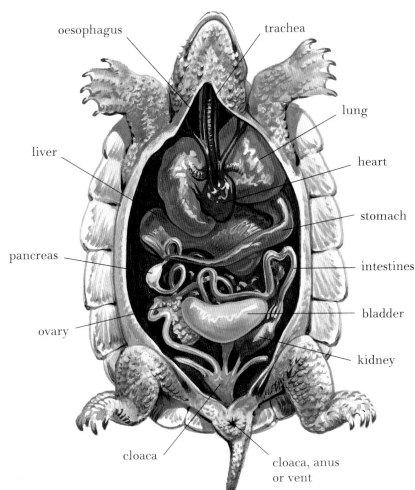

oesophagus trachea liver lung heart pancreas stomach intestines bladder ovary kidney cloaca cloaca, anus or vent

◀ TURTLE TAILS

Chelonian tails come in a variety of lengths and thicknesses, and are particularly long in snapping turtles. The big-headed turtle also has a long tail, which it uses as a brace to help it climb. Male chelonians (shown here on the left) often have longer and heavier tails than females (on the right), which usually have short, stubby tails. This is one way of telling the sexes apart.

SNORKEL NOSE ▶

Some freshwater chelonians, such as this snake-necked turtle, have a long neck and a tube-like nose that works like a snorkel. They can stay under water and just push their nostrils up above the surface to breathe air. As well as breathing air into their lungs, some freshwater chelonians also extract oxygen from the water. The oxygen is absorbed through areas of thin skin inside the throat and rear opening, or cloaca.

Temperature Check

Chelonians are cold-blooded. This does not mean that chelonians are cold. They need heat to keep their bodies working properly, but they cannot produce this heat themselves as mammals and birds do. Instead, their body temperature rises and falls with that of their surroundings. They control body temperature by basking in the sun to warm up and moving into the shade or water to cool down. In places with very cold or very hot seasons, chelonians may take shelter and go into a long sleep.

▲ CHILLY SWIMMER

The leatherback sea turtle swims farther into the cold northern and southern oceans than any other sea turtle. It has special ways of keeping warm in the cold water. Its dark body probably helps it to absorb the Sun's heat. The leatherback's muscles also produce heat, and this is trapped in the body by its thick, oily skin, which has a layer of fat underneath it. These turtles also have an ingenious system that keeps their flippers colder than the rest of the body, so heat is not lost as the turtle swims.

▼ SUNBATHING

On sunny days chelonians, such as these side-necked turtles, often bask in the sun to warm up. The extra warmth from the sunlight can speed up digestion and may help turtles to make Vitamin D, needed for healthy bones and shells. Females bask more than males because they need extra warmth for making eggs.

SUN SHELTER ▶

In hot climates, many land tortoises, such as this Mediterranean tortoise, need to shelter from the heat of the Sun. They seek out the shade cast by bushes or trees, or retreat into underground burrows. The tortoises dig out the burrows with their front legs, often making large chambers for resting or sleeping. Sometimes they sleep in their burrow throughout a hot season – this is called aestivation. The cool, moist tortoise burrows may also provide a refuge for other animals, such as mice, frogs and lizards.

◀ **HOW TO HIBERNATE**

Tortoises that sleep throughout the cold season in the wild also need to do so when in captivity. This deep winter sleep is called hibernation. Before hibernating your pet tortoise, make sure it is fit, has enough body fat and that there is no food in its gut. During hibernation, the tortoise must be dry and neither too hot nor too cold. To find out more, contact an organization such as the Tortoise Trust.

DRYING IN THE SUN ▶

A basking yellow-bellied turtle stretches its neck and legs and spreads its toes wide to soak up as much sunshine as possible. Basking makes a turtle drier as well as warmer. This may help it to get rid of algae and parasites growing on its shell. A thick covering of algae would slow the turtle's movement through the water, and it could also damage the shell.

Plodders and Swimmers

From slow, plodding land tortoises to graceful, swimming sea turtles, chelonians have developed a variety of types of legs and feet to suit their surroundings. On land, the heavy shell makes running impossible. It takes a land tortoise about five hours to walk just 1.6km (1 mile)! Sea turtles, with their powerful flippers, can reach the greatest swimming speeds of any living reptile. Some swim as fast as 30kph (20mph), which is as fast as humans can run on land. Freshwater chelonians have webbed feet for speed in swimming. Some chelonians make regular migration journeys to find food or nesting places.

▲ ELEPHANT LEGS
Land chelonians, such as this giant tortoise, have back legs like sturdy columns, which help to support them. The front legs may be like clubs or flattened and more like shovels, which helps with digging.

◄ FLIPPER FEET
The strong, flat flippers of sea turtles have no toes on the outside, although inside the flippers are five long toe bones bound together into one stiff unit. The front flippers are used to propel the turtle through the water, while the back ones act as rudders and brakes. There are only one or two claws on each flipper, and leatherback turtles have no claws at all. This makes the flippers more streamlined.

◄ SEASONAL WALKABOUT
Some freshwater chelonians, such as the spotted turtle (left) and wood turtle of North America, migrate on to land in the summer for feeding and nesting. In winter they return to swamps, pools and rivers to hibernate during the cold weather. On these short migrations, the turtles often have to cross roads. They run the risk of being run over, especially as they move so slowly.

WEBBED TOES ►
The feet of freshwater turtles have long toes joined together by webs, creating a bigger surface area to push against the water. They use all four legs to paddle along, but the back ones provide most of the pushing power. Freshwater chelonians also have gripping claws for walking on land and on the bottom of ponds and streams.

▲ FRESHWATER FLIPPERS
The pig-nosed turtle is the only freshwater turtle with flippers. Like a sea turtle, it flies through the water, moving both front flippers at the same time. Other freshwater turtles mainly use their back legs to swim, and move their front legs alternately. The pig-nosed turtle has two claws on the edge of each paddle-like leg. The back claws are used for digging nests.

Slow and Steady Winner
In Aesop's fable The Hare and the Tortoise *a speedy hare boasted about how fast he could run. He made fun of the tortoise, with his short feet and slow walk. But the tortoise just laughed and challenged the hare to a race. The hare thought there was no need to hurry because the tortoise was so slow. Instead of racing, he took a nap by the side of the road. The tortoise just kept plodding slowly along. As the tortoise approached the finish, the loud cheering woke up the hare, but he was too late to win the race.*

Eyes, Ears and Noses

A chelonian's most important senses are sight, taste and smell. The shell and skin are also sensitive to touch. Chelonians probably do not hear very well, although they can pick up vibrations through an ear inside the head. They do not have an ear opening on the outside of the head, as we do. Their eyesight is best at close-range, and they can see details. Good eyesight is useful for finding food, avoiding predators and navigating on long journeys. As well as smelling through their noses, chelonians have a structure in the mouth called the Jacobson's organ. This allows them to detect tiny chemical particles in the air.

▲ VIBRATION DETECTORS
The extraordinary matamata lives in murky waters where it is hard to see clearly. Its eyes are very small, and it does not seem to detect its prey by sight. Instead, it relies on the flaps of skin on its head, which have lots of nerve endings and are very sensitive to vibrations in the water. The flaps pick up signs of prey as the matamata moves through the water, and this helps it to get ready to attack.

Did you know? A chelonian can feel pressure on its shell just as you can on your fingernails.

◄ ON THE CHIN
Many freshwater turtles, such as this side-neck turtle, have fingers of skin, called barbels, dangling under their chins. Snapping turtles have four pairs. Scientists are not sure exactly what the barbels are for, but they seem to be sensory structures. Some Australian side-necks touch each other's barbels during their courtship display.

Robot Turtle

These girls are joining the electrical leads to a robot called a Turtle. Schoolchildren are able to instruct the Turtle robot to make simple movements and draw lines and patterns across a large sheet of paper. Inside the Turtle's see-through shell are the wheels it uses to move about. Working with the Turtle robot helps children learn how computers work and how to give them simple instructions.

▲ THE EYES HAVE IT

Sea turtles have good vision under the water but are short-sighted on land. Their large upper eyelids protect the eyes while they are swimming. Chelonians also have a third eyelid, called a nictitating membrane. This cleans the eye and keeps it moist, protecting it like a pair of goggles.

▼ TASTY TONGUE

A chelonian's tongue is broad and flat and firmly attached to the bottom of the mouth, which stops it from moving around. Taste buds on the tongue and in the throat are used for tasting food, although the sense of taste is also linked to the sense of smell. This leopard tortoise comes from Africa, and in the wild it eats grasses, prickly pear cacti and thistles.

▼ MR RED-EYE

Adult male box turtles often have red eyes, while the eyes of the females are yellow or brown. A few females also have red eyes, but they are less bright than the males'. Scientists have shown that turtles seem to prefer shades of orange and blue. Japanese turtles can even be trained to tell the difference between red and blue.

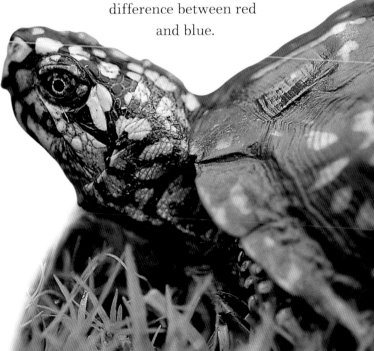

What Chelonians Eat

Chelonians may be herbivores (plant-eaters) or carnivores (meat-eaters), but many of them are omnivores, which means they eat all kinds of food. Some herbivores, such as the cooters of North and Central America, have jaws with jagged edges. This helps them to crush plant food, such as stems and fruits.

The diet of omnivores often changes with age. Young ones tend to eat more insects, while adults either eat more plants or have a more specialized diet. Many chelonians pick up extra nutrients by feeding on dung or dead animals. Also, after eggs have hatched, female offspring may eat the eggshells to help them build a store of calcium for producing the shells of their own eggs.

▲ GRASS FOR LUNCH
A giant Galapagos tortoise uses its horny jaws to bite off pieces of grass. Galapagos tortoises also eat other plants, such as cacti and other fleshy, water-filled plants. In the dry season, these tortoises have to get all their water from their plant food.

NOT A FUSSY EATER ▶
The hawksbill sea turtle is an omnivore that seems to prefer invertebrates (animals without backbones) such as coral, sponges, jellyfish, sea urchins, shrimp and molluscs. Plants in its diet include seaweeds and mangrove fruits, leaves, bark and wood. The hawksbill has a narrow head with jaws meeting at an acute angle. This helps it to reach into narrow cracks in coral reefs and pull out food.

▲ CHANGING DIET

Many chelonians, such as this slider, change their diet as they grow up. Young sliders eat more insects, while adults feed on mainly plants. Some chelonians switch to a whole new diet when they reach adulthood. When males and females are different sizes, they may also have different diets. Female Barbour's map turtles are more than twice the size of the males. They eat mainly shellfish, whereas the males feed mostly on insects.

OPEN WIDE ▶

Chelonians never need to visit the dentist, because they do not have teeth! Instead of teeth, their jaws are lined with hard keratin – the material fingernails are made of. The keratin is either sharpened into cutting edges or broadened into crushing plates. Cutting edges slice through animal bodies, while plates are used to grind plant food. Some ancient turtles had a set of teeth on the roof of their mouth, but did not have proper ones along the edges of the jaws, like most reptiles and other vertebrates.

Feeding Pets

Feeding pet tortoises or turtles is not as simple as you might think. An incorrect diet can lead to growth problems such as soft or deformed shells, and eggs with thin walls that break during laying. It is best to find out what your pet eats in the wild and try to feed it a similar, and varied, diet. Land chelonians eat mostly plants, while those that live in water have more animal food in their diets. High-fat foods, such as cheese, will make your pet overweight, and this is not good for its health. Ask the advice of an organization such as the Tortoise Trust for more information. Most pet chelonians need extra vitamins and minerals to make up for those missing in the prepared foods available from retailers. Water is important, too. Without enough to drink, your pet chelonian may suffer from kidney problems.

Turtle Hunters

Some chelonians have developed special hunting methods, such as lying in wait to ambush their prey or luring their prey towards them. Ambush hunters are usually well camouflaged and have long, muscular necks that can shoot out to grab a meal. Some turtles hide by flipping sand over their bodies or by burying themselves in soft mud. Most chelonians that live in water capture prey by opening their mouth wide and sucking in food and water.

The alligator snapping turtle lures its prey with a worm-like structure on its tongue. Common snapping turtles are more active hunters, grabbing small water birds. Other hunters herd fish into shallow water to make them easier to catch.

▲ **SNAKE STRIKE**

The common snake-necked turtle is named after its very long neck, which looks a little like a snake. The neck is more than two-thirds the length of the shell, which measures up to 28cm (11in) long. The snake-necked turtle creeps up on its prey and then lunges forward with its long neck, grabbing small creatures such as fish, frogs and worms, before they have time to escape.

BEWARE – AMBUSH! ▶

The spiny softshell turtle often buries itself in mud or sand with only its long head and neck showing. When small animals pass close by, the spiny softshell quickly shoots out its neck and gulps down its meal. To grab large prey, it may almost leap out of its hiding place, showering sand or mud everywhere. Spiny softshells feed on smaller water creatures, such as worms.

▲ SLOW FOOD

Few chelonians have the speed or agility to catch fast-moving prey. They usually eat slow-moving creatures, such as worms, insect grubs, caterpillars and molluscs. This Natal hinge-back tortoise is eating a millipede, which is not a speedy creature, despite having lots of legs. The long skull of this tortoise, with its sharp, hooked top jaw, helps it to reach out and grab prey.

▲ WORM DANCE

The wood turtle's omnivorous diet includes earthworms, which come to the surface of the ground after rain. Some wood turtle populations draw earthworms to the surface by stomping their feet to imitate the rain falling on the ground. A stomping turtle stomps with one foot and then the other at a rate of about one stomp per second for about 15 minutes or more. The loudest stomps can be heard 3m (10ft) away.

VACUUM MEALS ▼

The bizarre matamata from South America is a 'gape-and-suck' predator. It lies on the bottom of muddy rivers, moving so little that a thick growth of algae usually forms on its rough shell. It is so well camouflaged that small fish do not see it. When a fish swims close by, the turtle suddenly opens its huge mouth and expands its large throat, sucking the fish inside. All this happens at lightning speed, too fast for a human to see. The matamata then closes its mouth to a slit, flushing out the water but trapping its meal inside.

Focus on

Can you imagine savage turtles with bad tempers and jaws strong enough to bite off your fingers? The two kinds of snapping turtles of the Americas are just like this. The alligator snapping turtle is the heaviest freshwater turtle, growing to a length of 66cm (26in) and weighing as much as 80kg (176lb). The common snapping turtle is smaller, but still grows a carapace as long as 47cm (19in). Both kinds of snapping turtle live at the bottom of rivers and lakes. The common snapper is a prowling predator, stalking its prey with a slow-motion walk before grabbing it with a rapid strike. The alligator snapper sometimes hunts like this, but it usually sits with its mouth open and waits for food to swim into its jaws. Both of the snapping turtles are omnivores, eating algae and fruit, as well as lots of animals, from insects and crabs to fish and muskrats.

LURING PREY

The alligator snapping turtle has a red worm-like lure on its tongue. The turtle wriggles this 'worm' so that it looks alive. Hungry fish swim into the huge jaws to investigate the bait. The turtle then swallows small fish whole or pierces larger ones with the hooked tips of its strong jaws.

HANDLE WITH CARE

The common snapping turtle strikes with amazing speed, shooting out its head and biting with its sharp jaws. You can often hear the crunching sound as the jaws snap shut. It should only ever be approached by an expert, who will handle it only if absolutely necessary. When handled, these turtles also give off a musky scent.

Snapping Turtles

CRAFTY CAMOUFLAGE

The alligator snapping turtle is well camouflaged by its muddy-brown shell and skin. The bumps and lumps on its shell also help to break up its outline, so it is hard to see on the bottom of dark, slow-moving rivers. It keeps so still that a thick growth of algae usually grows on its rough shell, making it almost invisible to passing fish.

VARIED MENU

This snapping turtle is eating a young duck, but it is also strong enough to seize larger water birds by the feet and drag them under the water. Snapping turtles have a varied diet, which includes fish, dead animals, small water creatures and a surprising amount of plant material. The stomach of one snapping turtle caught in Columbia, South America, contained the remains of 101 freshwater snails.

BASKING BY DAY

During the day, the snapping turtle often floats beneath the surface of the water, with only its eyes and nostrils above the surface. It may also bask like this to warm up. If it is disturbed, the turtle can react with surprising speed. It is more active by night than during the day.

Courtship

Chelonians usually live on their own and meet only for mating. Depending on the environment, mating may occur all year round or just during agreeable seasons. The sexes are often difficult to tell apart, though they may be of different sizes or have tails of different lengths. Some males develop brighter markings on their body during the breeding season. Males seem to find their mates largely by sight, although some females, such as musk turtles, release scents to attract males. Some males bob their heads up and down or stroke the faces of females in an attempt to persuade them to mate. Females may also take part in the courtship dance.

▲ **FIGHTING FOR FEMALES**
Chelonians are aggressive fighters, and rival males, such as these desert tortoises, fight over females. They push, shove, bite and kick, sometimes wounding each other, until one gives up and beats a retreat. Sometimes one male flips his rival right over on to his back. It is difficult for upside-down chelonians to turn the right way up again. More often, the weaker male decides to beat a retreat rather than risk being injured by a stronger rival.

▼ **SIZE DIFFERENCE**
In this picture, which do you think is the male and which is the female? For many chelonians, the males and females are almost the same size. However, for nearly all land-living tortoises, females are larger than males. The small male leopard tortoise in the photograph is in fact chasing the larger female. In the case of giant tortoises and alligator snapping turtles, however, males are much larger than the females.

COURTSHIP DISPLAY ▼

Before chelonians mate, they may take part in a courtship dance. A male gopher tortoise, for example, bobs his head up and down and circles around the female. He bites her shell and legs (right) and crashes into her to try to force her to stand still for mating.

▼ MATING TIME

During mating, the male climbs on top of the carapace of the female. Males of many species have a hollow in the bottom of their shell, which fits around the female's shell. The male uses its claws to grip the female's shell. Many chelonians, such as these giant Galapagos tortoises, bellow and grunt during mating. In this case, the male is larger than the female and finds it difficult to heave himself into a mating position.

▲ CURIOUS CLAWS

Some male turtles, such as painted turtles, have three long claws on their front feet. Courtship begins with the male chasing the female through the water. When he overtakes her, the male turns to face the female and strokes her face with his claws. If the female wants to mate, she strokes the male's legs. The male then attempts to make the female follow him. She will sink to the bottom, where the pair mate.

LOOK AT ME ▶

In the breeding season a few males become much brighter to help them attract females. For example, male wood turtles develop bright orange skin on their neck and front legs. They pose in front of the females to show off their breeding signals, stretching out the neck and turning the head from side to side. Wood turtles also carry out a dance before mating. This involves walking towards each other and swinging their heads from side to side. The dance may go on for as long as two hours.

Eggs and Nests

All chelonians lay eggs on land because their young need to breathe oxygen from the air. Females usually dig a nest in sand, soil or rotting leaves. Apart from one species, the females do not stay to look after their eggs. The size and number of eggs vary enormously from species to species. Female African pancake tortoises lay one egg at a time, and giant Galapagos tortoises lay less than 15 eggs, but many sea turtles produce more than 100 eggs at a time. Several species may lay two or more clutches of eggs in one breeding season. The smallest eggs are less than 2.5cm (1in) in diameter, while the largest measure up to 7.6cm (3in).

▲ SANDY NESTS

Female sea turtles dig nests for their eggs on sandy beaches. Their eggs are soft and flexible, which means there is less danger of them cracking when they are dropped into the nest. Soft shells also use up less calcium and can absorb moisture. Young grow faster in soft shells than those in harder ones, which allows them to escape before beaches are flooded by the sea. Flooding kills the eggs because it cuts off the oxygen supply to the young.

◄ EGG LAYING

This Hermann's tortoise is laying her eggs in a hollow she has dug in the ground. The eggs have to fit through the opening at the back of her shell, so they cannot be too large. Larger females can lay bigger eggs. Many chelonians use their back legs to arrange the eggs as they are laid, sometimes into two or three layers separated by thin partitions of soil.

Did you know? A hawksbill turtle once laid as many as 258 eggs in just one clutch.

◄ ROUND EGGS

The red-footed tortoise lays round eggs with hard shells. Eggs with hard shells do not lose water as easily as those with soft shells. The round shape also helps to reduce water-loss because it has the minimum possible ratio of surface area to volume. In other words, there is less surface from which the liquid inside can leak out. Hard-shelled eggs are brittle, however, and are more likely to crack than soft-shelled ones. Giant tortoises produce sticky slime around their eggs to cushion the impact as they fall into a deep nest.

▼ GUARD DUTY

The Asian brown, or Burmese, tortoise is the only land species known to defend its nest. The female builds a large nest mound of dead leaves by sweeping the material backwards for up to 4m (13ft) around the nest. After she has laid her eggs, the female guards the nest for up to three days, which helps to protect the eggs from predators.

▲ CAPTIVE BREEDING

Many chelonians are bred in captivity. Most of these animals are sold as pets or for food so that they do not need to be taken from the wild. Captive breeding is also a good way of increasing the numbers of rare chelonians. Artificial incubators (above) copy the conditions inside nests, keeping the eggs warm and moist enough for proper development. In the case of chelonians, such as box turtles and most tropical tortoises, the developing embryo will die or be deformed if the eggs dry out too much.

Focus on Green

Green turtles breed for the first time when they are between 25 and 50 years old. When they are ready to mate, both males and females migrate from their feeding grounds to courtship areas close to nesting beaches. Nesting beaches are in warm places around the world, from Central America and the Pacific islands to the shores of Africa and South-east Asia. Some may travel as much as 2,000km (1,245 miles).

Green turtles nest every two or three years. They lay several clutches during a nesting year, about two weeks apart. A female comes ashore in the cool of the night to lay eggs, dragging herself slowly up the beach. After digging a pit with her flippers, she lays her eggs in it. Then she sweeps sand over her eggs and heads back to the sea.

MATING IN WATER

These green turtles are mating in water. Mating in the water is easier than on land because the water supports the weight of the male's body. This means he is not as heavy on top of the female. Males of many sea turtles have hook-like claws on their front flippers to grip the front edges of the female's carapace and help them stay in position while they mate.

DIGGING THE NEST

A female green turtle digs her nest on her own, using her front flippers at first to throw sand out of the way, then her back flippers to scrape out a hole. The nest is as deep as the length of the her back flipper. She lays about 120 eggs, which are the size of ping-pong balls. The whole process takes up to four hours, as many false nests may be dug and abandoned.

Turtle Nests

COVERING THE EGGS

When the female green turtle has finished laying her eggs, she disguises the nest chamber by sweeping sand into the hole. She uses all four flippers to do this, making a mound of sand. After kneading the sand mound for some time, the female throws sand over the spot again to make it hard for predators to find.

BACK TO THE SEA

After the female has hidden the nest as well as she can, she hauls her heavy body back down the beach to the sea, taking regular rests. She will have to crawl a long way because the nest must be far up the beach so that it is on dry sand, out of reach of the high tides.

HATCHING OUT

About two months after they are laid, the eggs hatch. The baby green turtles work together to dig out of the nest. It takes them three days to struggle out. Eventually, on a cool evening, the babies rush down to the sea, hoping to avoid falling prey to predators, such as raccoons.

SWIMMING BABES

Hatchlings that do manage to reach the sea dive into the waves and ride the undertow out to sea. They swim continuously for 24–48 hours until they reach deeper water, where they are less at risk from predators, such as sharks. Only one or two out of the clutch live long enough to breed.

Hatching and Young

▲ **BREAKING FREE**

The trigger for a baby chelonian to hatch is the need for more oxygen. A hatching turtle makes a hole in its shell using a sharp little scale called an egg tooth, on the tip of its snout. This falls off within a few weeks. As well as pushing at the shell with its egg tooth, the hatchling bites pieces from the shell and pushes with its legs. Escape can be a slow process, taking several hours.

The amount of time it takes for chelonian eggs to hatch varies enormously, but warmer temperatures speed up the process. For many chelonians, the temperature in the nest also determines the sex of the hatchlings. Higher temperatures tend to lead to more females being born. For some species, such as snapping turtles, however, both higher or lower temperatures than average produce more females. Species from cooler climates usually take from two to three months to hatch, whereas tropical species take from four months to over a year. The shortest incubation times are for the Chinese softshell (40–80 days) and the giant South American river turtle (50 days). The chelonian with the longest incubation time is the leopard tortoise of Africa. Its eggs take over a year to hatch.

A QUICK REST ▶

Once a hatching chelonian has opened the shell to allow oxygen to enter, it often stays in the egg for a day or more. This gives it time to grow stronger before escaping from the shell. A yolk sac, which has kept the baby alive during its development, provides a food reserve. You can see the pink yolk sac inside this shell. This is gradually absorbed into the hatchling's body in a few hours or days, giving it extra energy. Then the hatchling is able to move about easily.

34

▲ ESCAPE TUNNEL

For turtles that hatch in an underground nest, such as these olive Ridley sea turtles, the first thing they have to do is to reach the surface. Hatchling turtles are good at digging, but it may take the efforts of all the hatchlings in a nest to break free into the open air.

▲ FREE AT LAST

All hatchlings look like small adults and have to fend for themselves as soon as they hatch. When they are free of the nest, they have to find their way to a suitable habitat. For these leatherback turtle hatchlings, this is the sea. Freshwater turtles sometimes take several days to reach water. Both Blanding's turtle and wood turtle hatchlings follow the trails of others, perhaps picking up their scent.

▲ A BABY IN THE HAND

Baby chelonians are very tiny when they first hatch out. Most are just 30–40mm (1–1½in) long. These Australian snake-neck turtle hatchlings will easily fit on a person's hand. The one on the left is upside down and the one on the right is the correct way up.

▼ A BIT OF AN ARMFUL!

From left to right these young tortoises are: a red-footed tortoise, an Indian star tortoise, a leopard tortoise and an African spurred tortoise. Different species should not actually be kept together, since they have different habitats and diets and could give each other diseases they would not normally get in the wild. The African spurred tortoise will eventually grow much bigger than all the others – over twice as big as the star tortoise. Some chelonians stop growing when they become adults, but others keep growing throughout their lives.

Survival Games

Humans are probably the greatest threat
to chelonians, but other predators include
alligators, otters, eagles, bears, raccoons,
lizards and crabs. Big turtles, such as alligator
snappers and Mexican giant musk turtles,
also eat some of the smaller mud and musk
turtles. Chelonians have many ways of
defending themselves against predators.
The most obvious ways are withdrawing
into the shell, hiding or running away.
Vibrations in water or through the ground
warn of an approaching enemy, and some
chelonians can move away quickly if
necessary. Some young chelonians, with their
softer shells, have protective spines around
the edge of the shell. Few chelonians make
it to adulthood, but those who do can live
for a long time. Giant tortoises may live for
more than 200 years.

▲ STRONG SHELL
The ornate box turtle lives on
the vast grasslands or prairies
of central North America. It
sometimes eats the insects in
cattle dung and risks being
trampled by cattle hooves
as it searches for food. Its high,
domed carapace makes the shell
stronger, so it is harder to crush
than a more flattened shell.

CLEVER CAMOUFLAGE ▶
The pattern on a chelonian's
shell often provides good
camouflage, which helps it to
blend into the surroundings
and hide from predators. This
Central American wood turtle
is very hard to spot among the
surrounding brown leaves.
Even brightly marked
tortoises blend into their
natural background
surprisingly well, especially
when they keep still.

▲ STINKY TURTLE

Stinkpot turtles discourage predators
by giving off foul-smelling chemicals
from their musk glands – hence
their name. Other chelonians that use
stinky scent as a form to warn off
enemies include common
snapping turtles,
musk turtles,
helmeted terrapins
and the gibba
turtle from South
America.

Did you know? During hibernation, some species spend weeks under water without coming up for air.

▲ SHELL OPENER

Birds of prey, such as this golden eagle, have
developed a clever way of breaking open the tough
shell of tortoises. They pick the tortoises up in their
strong talons (claws) and drop them from a great
height on to hard stones or rocks. The force with
which the tortoises hit the hard surface may break
their shell open. The bird can then eat the soft fleshy
body inside the shell.

BUMPS AND SPINES ▶

Some turtles, such as sawback turtles
and spiny turtles (right), have bumps and
spines on their shells. The bumps of the
sawbacks help the turtles tilt the shell
to one side if they are flipped over on
to their back. This makes it easier for
the sawback to right itself again. The
spines along the edge of the shell of
spiny turtles, especially young ones,
probably help with camouflage by
breaking up the regular shape of the shell.
They also make it very difficult for predators,
such as snakes, to swallow them.

Focus on

Of the seven species of sea turtle, six have hard shells. These are the green, flatback, hawksbill, loggerhead, Kemp's Ridley and olive Ridley turtles. Most of these gentle and mysterious creatures are found in warm waters worldwide. The seventh sea turtle is the leatherback. This soft-shelled giant swims in both warm and cold ocean waters. Sea turtles use their strong flippers to 'fly' through the water. Only the females come on to land to lay their eggs. A male sea turtle may never touch dry land again after hatching from its egg and heading out to sea. In a few places, such as Hawaii, green turtles bask in the sun on beaches.

MYSTERIOUS LIVES

Once a loggerhead hatchling reaches the sea, its movements are not well known. In places such as Florida, they seem to rest on mats of floating seaweed (above). The babies are reddish brown above and below, which gives them good camouflage among the brown seaweed. This helps them to hide from predators.

BIGGEST CHELONIAN

This nesting turtle is being observed by a conservation scientist. The enormous leatherback is as long as a tall person and weighs around 659kg (1,450lb). It is the fastest growing of all chelonians, increasing its body weight by about 8,000 times between hatching and growing into an adult. Its shell has no horny scutes. Instead, it has a leathery skin with thousands of small bones embedded in it. It feeds on soft prey such as jellyfish.

Sea Turtles

NESTING TOGETHER

This olive Ridley turtle will join a large group for nesting. More than 100,000 females nest each year on the east coast of India alone. Most sea turtles nest alone or in small groups.

AFRICA

ASCENSION
ISLAND

SOUTH
AMERICA

MIGRATION OF
GREEN TURTLES

MIGRATIONS

Sea turtles, both young and adults, swim along ocean migration routes as they move to new feeding sites. Adults also travel to beaches to mate and lay eggs. Scientists are not sure how the turtles find their way. They may smell their route, find their way by the Sun or stars, or use Earth's magnetism.

STREAMLINED SHELL

Sea turtles, such as this green sea turtle, have a very streamlined shell to allow the water to flow smoothly over it. They do not have the overhang at the front of the shell, into which other chelonians withdraw their heads, as a ridge would slow a sea turtle down. Instead, its head is protected by thick, horny scales and the solid bony roof of the skull.

TORTOISESHELL

The scutes of the hawksbill turtle are a beautiful mixture of amber, brown, black, white, red and green. It is these scutes that are used to make 'tortoiseshell' combs, ornaments and spectacle frames. Sadly, the turtle is usually killed before the scutes are removed. This practice is entirely unnecessary, especially now that so many man-made alternatives are available.

Europe and the Mediterranean

Many tortoises from the area around the Mediterranean Sea belong to the *Testudo* group. This name comes from the Latin word for 'tortoise'. *Testudo* tortoises usually have five claws and all species except *Testudo horsefieldi* have a weak hinge on the plastron. Most tortoises in this group live in dry habitats, although some, such as the European pond turtle and the Spanish turtle, live in water habitats.

The Mediterranean region is a crowded part of the world, and the survival of many of the chelonians in this region is affected by the human population. They are threatened by habitat destruction, disturbance, pollution, summer fires and collection for the pet trade.

▲ POND LURKER

The European pond turtle is the only turtle to be found across Europe. A shy omnivore, the pond turtle lives in slow-moving waters with muddy bottoms and overhanging plants. Males have red eyes and longer tails than the yellow-eyed females.

◄ DRY DWELLER

Hermann's tortoise is found in dry places across southern Europe, from Spain to Turkey. It also lives on several Mediterranean islands. During the breeding season, rival males may become very aggressive and have shell-ramming contests with each other. The tortoises hibernate between October and April.

SCALY LEGS ▶

The spur-thighed tortoise is found around most of the Mediterranean region and in eastern Europe. In the cooler, northern parts of its range, the tortoise hibernates through winter. In warmer areas, it may be dormant in the hot summer. This is one of the most popular tortoises in the European pet trade, and many have been collected from the wild. Laws have now been passed to try to control this trade.

◀ MIDDLE EASTERN

The Egyptian tortoise lives in the deserts and scrublands of Libya, Egypt and Israel. It shelters from the heat in burrows. This is a very small species, with males having a carapace length of just 10cm (4in) and females being 13cm (5in) long, less than half the size of the marginated tortoise (below). Egyptian tortoises have a yellowish shell and spiky scales on each heel.

Did you know? Legend says that the Greek god Hermes made the first lyre from a tortoise shell.

LOOKING EDGY ▼

The marginated tortoise lives only in southern Greece and on some of its offshore islands. It has been introduced to Sardinia by people. This is the largest of the *Testudo* tortoises, with adults having a carapace length of up to 30cm (12in). Adults have a very distinctive fringe of flat scutes around the carapace, hence the name 'marginated', meaning 'around the edges, or margins'. Little is known about the habits of this tortoise, but it probably hibernates during the winter in cooler areas.

41

Africa and Madagascar

About 50 species of chelonian live in Africa south of the Sahara Desert and on the island of Madagascar, which lies off the East African coast. Madagascar is home to some interesting and rare tortoises that are found nowhere else in the world, such as the spider tortoise. Unusual chelonians from mainland Africa include the pancake tortoise, hinge-back tortoises and tent tortoises, with their unique shells. These tortoises are adapted to live in dry climates. Africa is also home to many side-necked turtles and softshell turtles, which live in ponds, rivers and marshes.

▲ BIG BURROWER

The African spurred tortoise has a shell that is 75cm (30in) long. Only the giant tortoises of the Galapagos Islands and Aldabra are larger. It lives along the southern edge of the Sahara Desert, in dry grasslands. To avoid the heat and dry air, it hides in burrows during the day and comes out at dusk and dawn, when it is cooler. This tortoise gets most of its water from its food.

▼ PRETTY PATTERNS

The beautiful radiated tortoise lives only in the dry woodland and scrublands of southern Madagascar. It is a relatively large species, growing up to 40cm (16in) long, with a highly domed carapace and a yellowish head. This tortoise lives a long time, with some individuals known to be well over 100 years old. Radiated tortoises are threatened by habitat destruction and other forms of interference, but they are being protected by law and bred in zoos around the world.

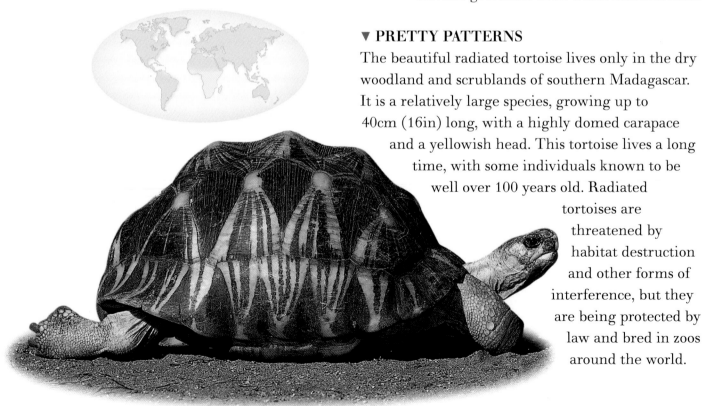

◄ A BUMPY ROOF

The spectacular African tent tortoise lives in southern Africa. It survives in various habitats ranging from sandy desert to bushy woodland. The shell varies in shape and pattern. One sub-species catches rain by tipping up the back part of its shell and stretching its front legs and head. Rain flows through the ridges of the shell into the mouth.

▼ CREEPY CRAWLIES

The little Malagasy spider tortoise is named after the pattern of yellow lines on its domed shell that looks like a spider's web. It is the only tortoise with a hinge at the front of the plastron so it can almost close the front of its bottom shell. The spider tortoise lives in forests along the south coast of Madagascar. It is a plant-eater, and it grows up to 15cm (6in) long.

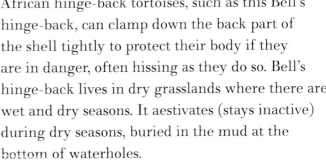

▲ SPECIAL SHELL

African hinge-back tortoises, such as this Bell's hinge-back, can clamp down the back part of the shell tightly to protect their body if they are in danger, often hissing as they do so. Bell's hinge-back lives in dry grasslands where there are wet and dry seasons. It aestivates (stays inactive) during dry seasons, buried in the mud at the bottom of waterholes.

GLORIOUS MUD ►

The West African mud turtle is a side-necked turtle and protects its head by tucking it to the side under its shell. This species lives in a variety of watery habitats, such as rivers, marshes and lakes. If the water dries up for part of the year, these turtles aestivate buried under the mud. The only turtles known to hunt in groups, they will attack and eat water birds.

Asian Chelonians

In many Asian cultures, chelonians are symbols of long life, strength, good fortune and endurance. Live tortoises were presented as gifts to Chinese emperors, and freshwater turtles still live in many temple ponds. Asians also hunt turtles and tortoises for food and for their bones. The bones are used in traditional remedies, especially in China. Unfortunately, many species of chelonians are now close to extinction because too many of them have been collected from the wild for use in these remedies, as well as for food or for sale as pets. Even though protected areas have been set up recently and wildlife protection laws are being enforced more strictly, Asian chelonians still face big survival problems in the future.

▲ DIGGING TORTOISE

Horsfield's tortoise lives further north than any other Asian tortoise. It ranges from Russia to Pakistan, in habitats that are hot in summer but freezing cold in winter. These tortoises dig burrows for shelter with their strong claws. There are laws protecting these tortoises, but they are still sold as pets in many parts of the world.

◄ TURTLE IN A BOX

The shy Malayan box turtle is found throughout South-east Asia. It lives in wetter habitats than the American box turtles, in ponds, marshes and flooded rice fields. This is one of the world's most popular pet species, and so many turtles have been captured from the wild that its numbers have been greatly reduced. This turtle feeds on both plant and animal foods when in captivity, and most likely lives on plants, small fish, water snails and insects in the wild.

▼ ROOFS AND TENTS

The Indian tent turtle belongs to a group of seven species with a carapace that looks like a tent or roof. It is shaped like an arch with a ridge, or keel, running along the middle, with points sticking up from the keel in several species. These Asian tent and roofed turtles look rather like the American sawback turtles. Their toes are webbed for swimming.

▲ RARE IMPRESSIONS

The rare impressed tortoise has an unusual flat carapace covered with scutes that have a dip in the middle. It lives in dry forests on hills in South-east Asia and China. These tortoises rely on heavy dew or wet plants for drinking water. They are very difficult to keep in captivity and are endangered due to hunting as well as habitat destruction.

▼ INDIAN FLAP-SHELL TURTLE

Hunted for its meat and for the pet trade, the Indian spotted flap-shell is gravely endangered. It is one of the smallest of the softshell turtles; males are only 15cm (6in) long. As with all softshells, there are three claws on each foot. This species lives in the shallow and still waters of rivers, marshes, ponds, lakes and canals. It aestivates during dry periods.

Tortoise Guardian

This bronze sculpture of a tortoise is in the Forbidden City in Beijing, China. The tortoise symbolized long life, wisdom and happiness for the emperors who ruled China. In Chinese mythology, the tortoise is one of four spiritual creatures, each guarding a direction of the compass. The tortoise is guardian of the north, a bird guards the south, a dragon guards the east and a tiger guards the west. These four animals also represent the four seasons – the tortoise represents winter. For over 4,000 years, tortoise shells have been used in Chinese rituals to foretell the future.

45

American Chelonians

North, Central and South America are home to a vast variety of chelonians, ranging from common species, such as cooters and sliders, to rarer species, such as the Arrau river turtle and the matamata. One species, the Central American river turtle, looks just like its relatives that lived millions of years ago. It is so well adapted to its underwater environment that it has not needed to change over time.

As with chelonians in many other places, American ones are threatened by hunting and habitat destruction. Galapagos tortoises have the added problem of goats, which were introduced to the islands by humans and compete with the tortoises for food.

▲ **TASTY TURTLE**
The chicken turtle used to be a popular food in the southern United States and gets its popular name from its succulent flesh. It is common in still water, such as ponds and swamps. In the wild, its shell often becomes thickly coated with algae.

COMMON COOTERS ▶
Cooters are large freshwater turtles with a carapace measuring up to 40cm (16in) long. Males are slightly smaller and flatter than females. They have long claws on the front feet which they use for stroking the female during their courtship display. Florida cooters like to bask in the sunshine, and groups of as many as 20 or 30 individuals may bask together. Each female lays two clutches of about 20 eggs each year, and the hatchlings are very brightly patterned.

▼ TWIST-NECKED TURTLE

The twist-necked turtle from northern South America is a side-necked turtle and lives in shallow rainforest streams and pools. It also wanders about the forest floor after rain. Since it is a poor swimmer, it does not live in large, fast-flowing rivers. The female does not dig a nesting hole, but lays one egg at a time under rotten leaves on the ground.

▲ SPINY SOFTSHELL

The habitat of the strange-looking spiny softshell turtle ranges across most of North America and down into Mexico. The round carapace measures about 50cm (20in) long and has a rough, leathery covering. The spiny softshell turtle spends most of its time in the water, often burying itself in sandy river bottoms. In shallow water, it may be able to stretch out its neck to breathe at the water's surface, while remaining hidden in the sand. Its prey includes fish, frogs and crayfish.

◄ HOOKED JAWS

The narrow-bridge musk turtle, from Central America, has several unusual features. One of the most obvious is the long hook on the bottom jaw and the tooth-like points on the top jaw. These formidable jaws help it to catch prey, such as frogs, fish and worms. Although quite shy, this turtle can give people a nasty bite if provoked. There are hardly any scales on the skin, and the plastron is very small, with only seven bones.

RED-FOOTED TORTOISE ►

Unlike most tortoises, the South American red-footed tortoise is very decorative, with bright red scales on the head, legs and tail and yellow spots on the shell. Males have longer, thicker tails than females. They also have a dip in the plastron, which helps them to climb on top of the more rounded female's carapace to mate. During mating, the males make clucking sounds.

Focus on

FOOD WITH DRINK

This desert tortoise is eating the fruit of a prickly pear cactus, a plant with a lot of water stored inside. Desert tortoises also eat wildflowers and grasses, often sniffing or sampling plants before they bite. Sometimes they eat soil, which provides the bacteria needed to help them break down their food. They swallow small stones, called gastroliths, which crush plant food as they churn round in the tortoise's stomach.

AMERICAN DESERTS

The desert tortoise of North and Central America lives in the Mojave and Sonoran deserts of south-eastern California, Arizona and Mexico. Today its habitat is under threat from land development, off-road vehicles and grazing farm animals. Many non-desert plants have taken root in the area. This is not good news for the tortoises, which need to feed on native plants to stay healthy.

Tortoises living in the deserts of North and Central America and Africa get most of their water from the plants they eat. They may also catch rainwater on their shell or dig basins to collect rainwater during showers. If water is not available, desert tortoises can absorb some of the water stored in their bladder. They may also survive a year or more without water. They tend to be active in the cool of the morning and evening. The hottest times of day, and very hot or cold seasons, are spent resting, aestivating or hibernating in underground burrows. These burrows are more moist and cooler than the surface of the desert.

Desert Tortoises

SUMMER SIESTA

The North American desert tortoise spends hot summer seasons, when food and water are hard to find, asleep in its burrow. During this 'summer sleep', or aestivation, the tortoise's body processes keep working normally, even though it hardly moves at all. This is different from its 'winter sleep', or hibernation, when its body processes slow down.

BORROWED BURROWS

The little Egyptian tortoise does not dig its own burrows, but uses burrows dug by rodents. This helps it to avoid hot temperatures. The Egyptian tortoise is rare, because it is threatened by the disturbance of its habitat. There are fewer and fewer bushes remaining, which are needed by desert rodents. This means there are fewer rodent burrows for the tortoise to shelter in.

CHAMPION DIGGER

The flattened, muscular front legs of the desert tortoise are brilliant tools for digging burrows that can be over 10m (33ft) long. The female uses her back legs for digging nest holes, too. She digs by scraping at the soil first with one leg and then the other. When the hole becomes deep enough, the tortoise turns around and pushes the dirt out with her shoulders.

Australasian Chelonians

Australia has been isolated from the rest of the world for millions of years, and this has allowed some rare and unusual species of chelonians to develop. The pig-nosed turtle is found only in this region, as are snake-necked turtles. Other chelonians in the same family as the snake-necked turtles include the river turtles and the snapping turtles of Australia and New Guinea. As with chelonians elsewhere in the world, many Australasian ones are very rare, but two species are especially so. The western swamp turtle lives only in pools near Perth, and the Fitzroy River turtle lives in only one river system in Queensland.

▲ SWIMMING PIG
An agile swimmer, the pig-nosed turtle has many unique features, including a pointed nose, a leathery shell and flipper-like limbs. It also has crescent-shaped scales along the top of its tail. The pig-nosed turtle rarely leaves the water but may bask on floating objects. It has a varied diet, including plants, insects and fish.

◄ SNAKE-NECKED TURTLES
With their extraordinary long necks, snake-necked turtles make rapid, snake-like strikes at their prey. They are active and very efficient predators, catching prey such as fish, shrimps, tadpoles and frogs. Some even manage to catch water birds. Like all side-necked turtles, snake-necked turtles tuck their long neck sideways under their shell to avoid danger or intense heat.

EASTERN TURTLE ▶

Basking on a log in the sun are two eastern river turtles, also called Brisbane short-necked turtles. They live in the east of Australia. Eastern river turtles have sensitive chin barbels and a yellow spot on each side of the chin. Adult males have flatter carapaces than females and longer, thicker tails.

◀ **SERRATED SNAP**

Beware of the serrated snapping turtle! It defends itself by snapping and biting and may also release a foul-smelling liquid from its musk glands. The serrated part of its name comes from the jagged edge on the back of its carapace. Younger ones have a ridge, or a keel, along the top of their shell. The serrated snapping turtle is a side-necked turtle, but it has a much shorter neck than its close relatives the snake-necked turtles. Males have much longer tails than females.

Aboriginal Art

This tortoise was painted on the rocks by Aboriginal people in Kakadu National Park, northern Australia. Aboriginal rock art can be up to 40,000 years old and was painted for a number of reasons, such as to ensure a successful hunt, to record ceremonies, to change events and people's lives through sorcery and magic, and to tell stories about the Creation Ancestors. Long ago, during the 'Dreamtime', these ancestors were believed to have created the landscape and every living creature before changing into land forms, animals, stars or other objects. The act of painting puts artists in touch with their Creation Ancestors and is seen as an important and powerful experience in itself.

Ancient Chelonians

▲ FORMING FOSSILS

This fossil tortoise was found in the badlands of South Dakota, in the United States. It lived about 35 million years ago, when that area was covered in a shallow sea. Rock and minerals have filled in the spaces inside the tortoise's shell and then turned into hard stone, preserving the tortoise's body for millions of years.

Scientists have different ideas about which group of animals chelonians evolved from. The oldest known chelonian, called *Odontochelys*, lived about 220 million years ago, but this ancient turtle probably did not give rise to modern chelonians. These are most likely to have developed from a group called the Casichelydia, which lived between 208 and 144 million years ago. Ancient chelonians lived alongside the dinosaurs – giant reptiles that roamed the Earth until 65 million years ago, when they all died out. Unlike the dinosaurs, many chelonian species survived and are still around today.

► LARGEST TURTLE

About 100 million years ago there was an ancient turtle called *Archelon*, which was bigger than a rowing boat. It swam in an inland sea that once covered the grassy prairies of North America. *Archelon* looked like modern leatherback turtles, with a leathery, streamlined carapace and wing-like front flippers. It had very weak jaws and may have fed on jellyfish and other animals with soft bodies, such as squid. The most complete fossil of *Archelon* is of an animal that was about 100 years old when it died. It was 4.5m (15ft) long and 5.25m (17ft) from one outstretched front flipper to the other.

Triassic 252–201mya	Jurassic 201–145mya	Cretaceous 145–66mya	Paleocene to present 66mya–present		mya – millions of years ago
				Kinosternidae	Mud or musk turtles
		Trionychoidea (Cretaceous–recent)		Dermatemydidae	Central American river turtle
Odontochelys (extinct)				Carettochelyidae	Pig-nosed turtle
	Cryptodira (Late Jurassic)		Chelonioidea (Jurassic–recent)	Trionychidae	Softshell turtles
				Dermochelyidae	Leatherback turtle
	Casichelydia (dominant during Jurassic)			Cheloniidae	Sea turtles
		Testudinoidea (Paleocene–recent)		Chelydridae	Snapping turtles
				Platysternidae	Big-headed turtle
				Emydidae	Pond turtles and relatives
		Pleurodira (Late Cretaceous–recent)		Testudinidae	Land tortoises
				Chelidae	Austro-South American side-necked turtles
				Pelomedusidae	African side-necked turtles

▲ EVOLUTION PATHWAYS

This diagram shows how chelonians may have evolved over a period of 220 million years. A group called the Casichelydia became dominant about 208 million years ago and gave rise to the 12 families of chelonians alive today. They are listed to the top right of the chart above.

Island Evolution

On the Galapagos Islands the English scientist Charles Darwin found some of the most important evidence for his theory of how evolution happens. During his visit in 1835 he collected information about how the giant tortoises and other animals varied between islands. He suggested that these differences had come about because the animals had adapted to suit the unique conditions on each island.

The best-adapted animals survived to produce the next generation, an idea that Darwin called 'natural selection'.

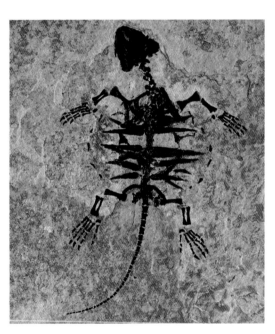

▲ SNAPPING FOSSILS

This is a fossil of a young snapping turtle that lived between 58 and 37 million years ago. You can see the outline of its shell and its long tail. From fossils, we know that there were more species of snapping turtles in the past. Today only the common snapping turtle and the alligator snapping turtle are still alive.

53

Living Relatives

The closest relatives of chelonians alive today are other reptiles, a name that means 'creeping creatures'. Reptiles have a bony skeleton, a backbone and scaly skin. They rely on their surroundings for warmth and are most common in warmer places. Reptiles lay eggs with waterproof shells or give birth to live young. The main groups of living reptiles are: turtles and tortoises, lizards and snakes, and crocodiles and alligators. Chelonians look very different from other reptiles. They also have no holes in the roof of their skull, while all other reptiles have two openings there.

▲ LEGLESS WONDER
With their long and slender, bendy bodies, snakes, such as this rattlesnake, look nothing like chelonians, despite evolving from a common ancestor. They have no legs, no eyelids and no external ears. Snakes have a forked tongue for tasting and for smelling the air. All snakes are meat-eaters and swallow their prey whole. They evolved much later than chelonians, between 100 and 150 million years ago, but have developed into many more species – about 2,700 different kinds in total.

▼ AMAZING ALLIGATORS
Alligators are large and fierce predators that belong to the crocodilian group of reptiles, which includes 13 species of alligator, crocodile, caiman and gharial. These long-snouted monsters have powerful jaws lined with sharp teeth. They are all meat-eaters, tackling prey of all sizes from fish to zebras. Although they live in or near fresh water or the sea, crocodilians must lay their eggs on land, just like chelonians.

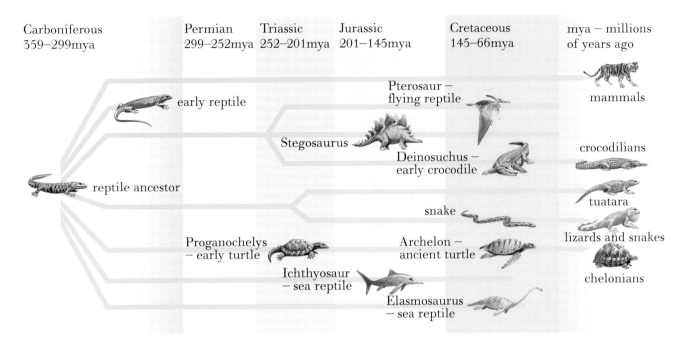

Carboniferous 359–299mya	Permian 299–252mya	Triassic 252–201mya	Jurassic 201–145mya	Cretaceous 145–66mya	mya – millions of years ago

early reptile

reptile ancestor

Pterosaur – flying reptile

Stegosaurus

Deinosuchus – early crocodile

snake

Proganochelys – early turtle

Archelon – ancient turtle

Ichthyosaur – sea reptile

Elasmosaurus – sea reptile

mammals

crocodilians

tuatara

lizards and snakes

chelonians

▲ REPTILE EVOLUTION

The first reptiles evolved from amphibians about 300 million years ago and looked like small lizards. About 220 million years ago, chelonians appeared and branched away from the other reptiles. These others then divided into two main groups: snakes and lizards, and the archosaurs, which includes dinosaurs, crocodiles and extinct flying reptiles called pterosaurs.

▲ LOTS OF LIZARDS

There are more species of lizard than any other group of reptiles – over 4,000 of them. This is a very unusual lizard from the Galapagos Islands. It is an iguana that lives on the seashore and dives under the water to graze on seaweed.

LIVING FOSSIL ▼

The tuatara is an unusual reptile that has changed so little since the days of the dinosaurs that people refer to it as a 'living fossil'. Today there are just two species of tuatara, living on islands off the coast of New Zealand. They are burrowing reptiles that live in coastal forests and come out at night. Tuataras live for a long time, probably over 100 years. This long lifespan is something they have in common with chelonians.

Chelonians and People

People are not good news for chelonians. They destroy, build on and pollute the places where these reptiles live. People also often introduce new animals into their habitats, such as goats and rats, that eat all the chelonians' plant food or eat their eggs. Chelonians are also caught for food or killed in fishing nets by accident. Their shells and skins are used to make trinkets, and other body parts are used in medicines. When people handle chelonians, they may pass on diseases that kill them. Catching wild chelonians to sell as pets reduces the numbers left in the wild, and many die before they reach the shop. Some pets are also neglected and do not live long.

▲ NO PLACE TO LIVE
The places where chelonians once lived are fast disappearing, as human populations expand rapidly and towns, roads and farms replace natural habitats. Many chelonians are run over as they plod their way slowly across roads. Desert tortoises are threatened by off-road vehicles. Even in the oceans, oil rigs and boat traffic badly affect sea turtles.

FOOD AND HUNTING ▶
Chelonians are relatively easy for people to catch as they move so slowly. Some traditional hunters, such as this San woman from southern Africa, use the meat as an important food source for their families. Catching small numbers is not a problem, however, as enough survive to replace those caught. Over-hunting to sell chelonians for high prices as gourmet food, for tortoiseshell or as live specimens to animal collectors is still a big problem. Much of the hunting is illegal and hard to control.

◄ CAUGHT IN THE NET

Commercial fishing nets often scoop up sea turtles, such as this baby hawksbill, as they are pulled through the oceans. The turtles become entangled in the nets and are strangled or drown, since they cannot reach the surface to breathe air. In 1999, 150,000 turtles were killed in this way by the shrimp-fishing industry all over the world. Sea turtles also get tangled up in long-lines, which are deep-water fishing lines many miles long with thousands of baited hooks.

PET CHELONIANS ►

Many people like to keep chelonians, such as land tortoises or terrapins, as pets. This is, however, not a decision to be taken lightly, as they can live for a very long time. They also need to be treated with care and respect and given appropriate food and housing. People can also pick up some diseases from chelonians, and vice versa. Most turtles in the pet trade are still taken from the wild, although some are bred in captivity, such as these baby wood turtles.

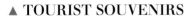

▲ TOURIST SOUVENIRS

In some countries, turtles and tortoises are still killed and their shells are made into souvenirs. The skin of Pacific and olive Ridley turtles is used to make soft leather items. The rest of the turtle is thrown away or used for pet food, hot dogs or fertilizer. If people stopped buying products made from turtles and tortoises, then this sad, and often illegal, industry would end.

▼ EGGS FOR SALE

These green-turtle eggs are being sold in a market in Malaysia. They cost more than chicken eggs, and in some areas they are used in love potions. If too many eggs are taken from the wild, there will not be enough baby turtles for the future.

Focus on

Turtles and tortoises are in terrible trouble. Populations nearly everywhere are shrinking, and many species are threatened or vulnerable. Over half of the world's chelonians are currently facing the threat of extinction, and unless we do more to save them now, countless species will be lost in the near future. Chelonians have no way of defending themselves against people, and they are too easy for us to catch. Females nest only in certain areas and at regular times, so people can easily harvest their eggs and young. Since they grow so slowly and take a long time to mature and reproduce, it is difficult for chelonians to build up their numbers again once they have been reduced to low levels.

ANGONOKA TORTOISE

This is one of the most endangered species in the world. Only a few hundred individuals survive in one area of Madagascar. These rare animals are now being bred in zoos around the world.

AFRICAN RARITY

The beautiful geometric tortoise has lost 96 per cent of its habitat because of agriculture, development and frequent wildfires. It was once more widespread but now lives in the south-western tip of South Africa. Here it inhabits isolated patches of a unique mixture of grasses and short, dry shrubs, which grow on acidic, sandy soils.

Rare Chelonians

ENDANGERED EUROPEAN

For centuries European pond turtles have been captured for food or destroyed because people considered them harmful to fish. Recent problems facing these turtles include pollution and the building of embankments along waterways, which stop the turtles from moving about freely to find food or mates.

SMUGGLING TORTOISES

Despite its name, the Egyptian tortoise is almost extinct in Egypt. Even though there are laws banning selling these tortoises, smuggling still occurs. This tortoise is rare not only because of habitat destruction and disturbance but also because of pet traders collecting them from the wild.

PROTECTING PANCAKES

The increasingly rare pancake tortoise lives only in Kenya and Tanzania in East Africa. It is threatened by people using its habitat for farming and by poaching for the pet trade. Even though these tortoises are protected by law and Kenya bans their export, smuggling occurs. Many of these unusual tortoises have died on journeys to other parts of the world. Since pancake tortoises lay only one egg at a time, it is hard for them to replace their numbers if too many are taken from the wild.

▲ PROTECTED BREEDING

On this Malaysian beach, the sticks mark the positions of leatherback turtle eggs buried in the sand. Within this protected area, the eggs are cared for and the hatchlings are helped on their journey to the sea. Populations of leatherbacks have declined drastically. The causes include people taking eggs from nests, and adults being caught in fishing nets at sea.

Conservation

Even though chelonians have survived on the Earth for hundreds of millions of years, their future survival is uncertain. We need to find out much more about how they live in the wild, so that we can work out the best ways to help them. One thing we do know for sure is that they need all the help they can get. Conservation measures to help chelonians include preserving their habitats, stopping illegal poaching and smuggling, controlling the pet trade, and breeding rare species in captivity so that they can be released back into the wild. Many countries have laws to protect chelonians, but these are difficult to enforce, especially in developing countries with fewer resources.

GATHERING DATA ▶

The loggerhead migrates thousands of miles each year, but scientists are not sure how it finds its way. The transmitter fixed to the shell of this loggerhead turtle will allow scientists to track its movements through the ocean. Every time the turtle comes to the surface for air, a signal is sent via a satellite to a research team. This tells the scientists where the turtles are, what the water temperature is and so on. Transmitters fixed to land chelonians are also providing information about how these tortoises live. The data gathered can be used to help protect species and preserve their limited habitats.

TORTOISE TRUST ▶

Organizations such as the Tortoise Trust campaign for the protection of turtles and tortoises around the world. The Tortoise Trust is the world's largest

chelonian organization, active in more than 26 countries. It gives advice on how to care for pet chelonians, promotes research and helps to find good homes for turtles and tortoises in need.

▲ **BROUGHT UP SAFELY**

Captive breeding of seriously endangered species, such as this Australian western swamp tortoise, may be the only way to save them from extinction. It is not always easy to breed chelonians in captivity, as they may suffer from stress and disease. Even if the breeding scheme is a success, there may not be a suitable area of their wild habitat left to release them into once they are mature.

▼ **ECO-TOURISM**

In some places tourists can help to save rare chelonians by going to watch them, as these tourists are doing in the Galapagos Islands. The money they pay can go towards conservation schemes. These tourists must be carefully controlled so they do not upset the chelonians or pass on any diseases. Unfortunately, the noise and disruption from tourists on sea turtle nesting beaches can confuse and disturb females so that they go back to sea without laying their eggs.

▼ **CONTROLLING TRADE**

The international pet trade condemns many chelonians to a slow and miserable death after collecting them from the wild. They are often packed tightly together in crates, such as this one seized by customs officials in Vietnam. With hardly any space, and no food or water, a large number of animals die during their journey.

GLOSSARY

aestivation
A period of rest during heat and drought, similar to hibernation.

bacteria
A large group of microscopic, single-celled living organisms.

barbel
A sensitive finger of skin under the chin of some chelonians.

bask
To lie for some time in the warmth of the Sun, like a person sunbathing.

camouflage
Coloration, patterns or shapes that allow an animal to blend in with its surroundings.

carapace
The top part of a chelonian's shell.

Carettochelyidae
A chelonian family with only one species, the pig-nosed turtle.

carnivore
An animal that eats meat.

Chelidae
A family of side-necked turtles from South America and the Australia-New Guinea region.

chelonians
Reptiles with bony shells and sharp, horny jaws. The term includes all turtles, tortoises and terrapins.

Cheloniidae
A chelonian family that contains six species of sea turtles: green, flatback, loggerhead, Kemp's Ridley, olive Ridley and hawksbill.

Chelydridae
A family of snapping turtles, which contains two species: the alligator snapping turtle and common snapping turtle.

cloaca
An opening at the back of a chelonian's body through which waste and eggs leave the body and mating takes place.

clutch
Eggs laid and incubated together.

cold-blooded
An animal whose body temperature varies according to its surroundings.

conservation
Protecting living things and helping them to survive in the future.

courtship
Ritual displays that take place before mating.

Dermatemydidae
A chelonian family with only one species, the Central American river turtle.

Dermochelyidae
A chelonian family that has only one species, the leatherback sea turtle.

digestion
The process by which food is broken down and absorbed into the body.

dinosaurs
An extinct group of reptiles that lived from 245 to 66 million years ago and dominated life on Earth.

egg tooth
A small, sharp point on the tip of a baby chelonian's snout, which helps it to break free from its eggshell.

Emydidae
A large and varied family of pond turtles including: the painted terrapin, spiny turtle, Indian tent turtle, wood turtle and diamond-back terrapin.

endangered species
A species that is likely to die out in the near future.

evolution
The process by which living things change over many generations.

extinction
When a species dies out.

flipper
A leg that has adapted into a flat blade for swimming.

fossils
The preserved remains of living things, usually found in rocks.

gastrolith
Hard objects, such as small stones, swallowed by some chelonians, which stay in the stomach and help to crush food.

habitat
The kind of surroundings in which an animal usually lives.

herbivore
An animal that eats plants.

hibernation
A period of rest during cold weather when an animal's body processes all slow down to save energy.

incubation
Keeping eggs warm so that the young will develop properly.

invertebrate
An animal without a backbone, such as a fly, worm, shrimp or snail.

Jacobson's organ
Nerve pits in the roof of the mouth that are sensitive to scent particles.

keratin
A horny substance that makes up the scutes of chelonians, the scales of lizards and snakes, and human fingernails and hair.

Kinosternidae
A chelonian family of mud and musk turtles including: the loggerhead musk turtle and narrow-bridged musk turtle.

migration
A regular journey to find food, water or a place to breed or lay eggs.

molluscs
Invertebrates with hard shells, such as mussels, clams or snails.

navigating
Finding the way to a certain place.

nictitating membrane
A third eyelid that can be passed over the eye to protect it.

omnivore
An animal that eats all kinds of food, both plants and animals.

palate
The roof of the mouth.

Pelomedusidae
A family of side-necked turtles found in South America, Madagascar, Africa and the Seychelles, including: the West African mud turtle, African forest turtle and giant South American river turtle.

plastron
The flat, bottom part of a chelonian's shell.

Platysternidae
A chelonian family with just one species, the big-headed turtle.

poaching
Capturing or killing animals illegally and selling them.

predator
An animal that catches or kills other animals for food.

prey
An animal that is hunted and eaten by other animals.

reptile
A scaly, cold-blooded animal with a backbone, including tortoises, turtles, snakes, lizards and crocodiles.

scutes
Horny scales that cover the shells of chelonians and the bodies of crocodilians.

species
A group of animals that share similar characteristics and can breed together to produce fertile young.

streamlined
A smooth, slim shape that cuts through air or water easily.

succulents
Plants such as cacti, which store water in their stems and leaves.

Testudinidae
A chelonian family of land tortoises, including: the leopard tortoise, Galapagos giant tortoise, impressed tortoise and radiated tortoise.

Trionychidae
A chelonian family of soft-shelled turtles including: the Florida softshell turtle, spiny softshell turtle and Zambezi flapshell turtle.

yolk sac
A bag of food inside an egg that nourishes a developing embryo.

Picture Acknowledgements
Corbis: 8t, 9t, 9c, 11l, 11tr, 12b, 16t, 19tl, 19br, 20t, 21bl, 24b, 25tl, 25b, 29l, 31c, 33tl, 38b, 45br, 50t, 51c, 51b, 52, 53l, 56b, 58t, 59tl, 61bl, 61tr; **Mary Evans Picture Library**: 5tl, 13br; **Chris Mattison**: 5cr, 7b, 12c, 15r, 17c, 25tr, 42t, 55t, 60t, 63t; **Bill Love**: 8b, 9b, 13tr, 15l, 19bl, 19tr, 23t, 23c, 35bl, 35br, 37b, 43t, 45l, 46, 47bl, 62; courtesy of Marc Cantos, Burgundy Reptiles: 29br, 57tr; **Natural History Picture Agency**: 3t, 4t, 6b, 7t, 21tr, 26t, 27, 39l, 42b, 43br, 44b, 47tl, 48b, 64t; **Nature Picture Library**: 1, 2b, 3b, 5tr, 7c, 10, 22, 23b, 26b, 28, 30t, 32t, 33b, 34b, 35tl, 37tr, 38t, 41t, 48t, 49t, 53r, 54b, 55b, 57tl, 57br, 64b; **Mark O'Shea**: 39br; **Oxford Scientific Films**: 2t, 4b, 5bl, 6t, 16b, 17b, 18, 33tr, 35tr, 39tr, 51t, 54t, 63b; **Science Photo Library**: 12t, 21tl, 24t, 32b, 60b; **Tortoise Trust**: 2cr, 5br, 11b, 13tl, 13bl, 17t, 20b, 21br, 29tr, 30b, 31t, 31b, 34t, 36, 37l, 40t, 41c, 41b, 43bl, 45tr, 47tr, 47br, 49b, 49r, 50b, 56t, 57bl, 58b, 59tr, 59b, 61tl; **Turtle Conservation Centre (Vietnam)**: 61b.

INDEX

Details of the Tortoise Trust and its work can be found on its website: www.tortoisetrust.org